Wonders

Program Authors

Diane August

Donald R. Bear

Janice A. Dole

Jana Echevarria

Douglas Fisher

David Francis

Vicki Gibson

Jan Hasbrouck

Margaret Kilgo

Jay McTighe

Scott G. Paris

Timothy Shanahan

Josefina V. Tinajero

Mc
Graw
Hill
Education

Cover and Title pages: Nathan Love

www.mheonline.com/readingwonders

Copyright © 2017 McGraw-Hill Education

All rights reserved. No part of this publication may be
reproduced or distributed in any form or by any means, or
stored in a database or retrieval system, without the prior
written consent of McGraw-Hill Education, including, but not
limited to, network storage or transmission, or broadcast for
distance learning.

Send all inquiries to:
McGraw-Hill Education
2 Penn Plaza
New York, NY 10121

ISBN: 978-0-07-678697-8
MHID: 0-07-678697-8

Printed in the United States of America.

2 3 4 5 6 7 8 9 RMN 20 19 18 17 16

A

Unit 8 From Here to There

The Big Idea: Where can you go that is near and far?

(t) Ed Meyer; (c) Mike Byrne; (b) StockTreck/Photodisc/Getty Images

Essential Question

What can help you go from here to there?

Go Digital!

Moving Along!

Talk About It

How does this child move from place to place?

Daniel MacDonald/Flickr/Getty Images

Say the name of each picture.

1

2

Read each word.

3   **jam**   **jig**   **jot**

4   **quit**   **quack**   **quick**

(t)RubberBall Productions/Getty Images; (tr)Joshua Ets-Hokin/Photodisc/Getty Images; Nathan Jarvis

here

me

Here comes the bus!

A jet will take **me** home.

(t)Frank Whitney/Photographer's Choice/Getty Images; (b)©David Frazier/Corbis

Dad Got a Job

Ed Meyer

Dad got a job at a dock.
We had to pack up.

Ed Meyer

Ed Meyer

"Pack with **me**," Dad said.
We can set up a big box.
I pack my red hat.

10

Tug! Tug! Lug! Lug!
"Jam it in," said Dad.
I quit on box six!

Ed Meyer

A big box can fit in a van!
We did it! We did it!

Ed Meyer

We had to get on a bus.
A quick bus got us to a jet.

Ed Meyer

13

We got on a quick jet!
Jack did not sit with me.
Jack had to sit in a bin.

Ed Meyer

We got in a tan cab.
Here is the dock!
"Not bad, Dad!" I said.

Ed Meyer

Dad Got a Job

Dad got a job at a dock.
We had to pack up.

Pages 8–15

Write About the Text

Amy

I responded to the prompt: **Write a journal entry from Dad's point of view. Tell how he feels about moving.**

Student Model: *Narrative Text*

Details
I used story details to tell what Dad does first.

I am happy I have a new job.

But, I have a lot to move.

First I pack up boxes.

I feel very tired.

Then I feel happy that
the boxes fit in the van!

SazzyB/iStock/Getty Images Plus/Getty Images

Grammar

The word **to** is a **preposition** in this sentence.

Reaction
I told how Dad felt when he got to his new place!

Next, I take a bus to a jet.

I fly on a jet.

Last I take a cab.

I am excited to get to the new place!

Your Turn COLLABORATE

Write a journal entry from the girl's point of view. Tell how she feels about moving near the dock.

Go Digital!
Write your response online.
Use your editing checklist.

17

Essential Question

What do you know about our country?

Go Digital!

The American Way

COLLABORATE

Talk About It

Why is this statue important to us?

MATTES Reñá©/hemis.fr/Getty Images

Say the name of each picture.

1

2

Read each word.

3 **yes** **yam** **yet**

4 **zip** **zig-zag** **Zack**

(t)D. Hurst/Alamy; (tr)Image State/Alamy; Nathan Jarvis

| this | what |

I was on **this** street.

What do zebras eat?

(t)Philip Coblentz/age fotostock; (b)ImageBroker/Alamy

Pack a Bag!

Mike Byrne

"Pop is here," said Zeb.
"Can I pack a big bag?"
Mom and Dad said, "Yes."

Mike Byrne

Zeb can get on a big jet.
He can zip to Pop.
Zeb is not sad!

Mike Byrne

What can Zeb see?
Zeb can nod at a man.
Zeb can see a big, big sun.

Mike Byrne

25

It was a quick, quick jet!
Zeb and Pop hug.
Pop got **this** pack for Zeb.

Mike Byrne

Pop and Zeb get up at six.
Pop can go up, up, up.
Zeb can go up, up, up.

Mike Byrne

Pop can zig-zag.
Zeb is hot and not quick.
"Do not quit yet!" said Pop.

Mike Byrne

Yes! They get to the top.
Zeb did it. Pop did it.
Zeb can sit and sip.

Mike Byrne

Write About the Text

Pack a Bag!

"Pop is here," said Zeb.
"Can I pack a big bag?"
Mom and Dad said, "Yes."

Pages 22-29

John

I answered the question: **How does Zeb feel about going out west? How do you know?**

Student Model: *Informative Text*

Zeb is excited to go out west.
He has packed a big bag.
He is showing Mom and Dad
a picture of a map.
He is not afraid to say good-
bye to Mom.

Clues
I used picture details to figure out that Zeb feels excited.

Jetta Productions/Blend Images/Getty Images Plus/Getty Images

Sentences

I wrote short and long sentences to make my writing interesting.

Zeb is smiling and waving to Mom.

He does not look scared.

Zeb looks excited to go on the plane.

He is smiling!

Grammar

The word **on** is a **preposition** in this sentence.

Your Turn

COLLABORATE

How do the author and illustrator show you that Zeb enjoyed his trip out west?

Go Digital!
Write your response online.
Use your editing checklist.

31

Essential Question

What do you see in the sky?

Go Digital!

COLLABORATE

Talk About It

What do you see in the night sky?

Evgeny Kuklev/Vetta/Getty Images

High in the Sky!

Review Letter Sounds

Say the name of each picture.

1.

2.

Read each word.

3. **up   gas   fox   jug**

4. **quick   yak   zig-zag   wax**

Nathan Jarvis

Review Words

Read the words and sentences.

1. for have they of

2. said want here me

3. this what

---

4. I **have** **this** box **of** crayons.

5. "**What** do you **want** to read?"

6. They can stay **here** with **me**.

Dave King/Dorling Kindersley/Getty Images

35

Up! Up! Up!

©UVimages/amanaimages/Corbis

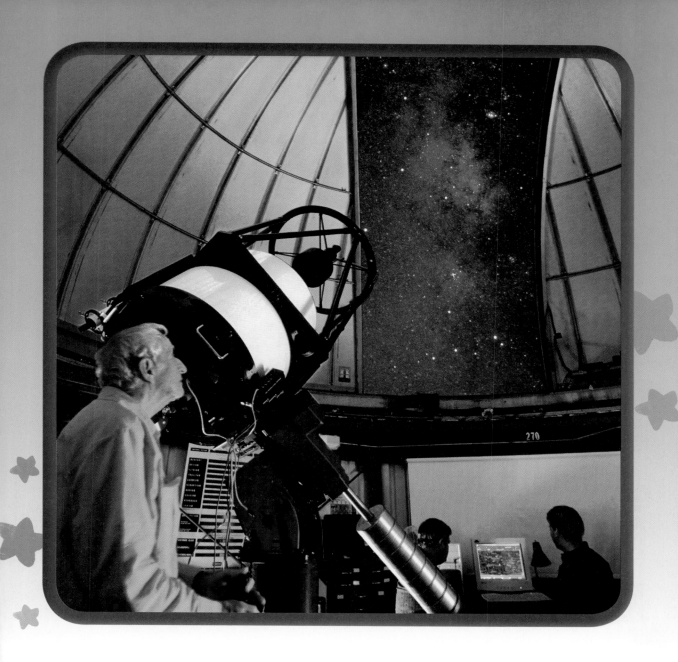

I **have** a fun job **here**.
I am in luck.
I can see up, up, up!

Photo Researchers/Getty Images

This is **what** I can see.

A jet can dip.

It can zip up, up, up!

©David Frazier/Corbis

Photodisc/Eyewire/Getty Images

Yes, a sun is big.
A sun can get hot.
I bet it can get up.

Gerard Lordriguss/Photo Researchers/Getty Images

I can see a big cup.
I can see a little cup.
Yes, **they** are up!

See up, up, up!
Is a dim dot on it?
Yes, it is a dot!

©Royalty-Free/Corbis

StockTreck/Photodisc/Getty Images

It is a bit **of** rock and gas.

I **want** to see it zig-zag.

I can see it up, up, up!

I can see up, up, up.
It is a fun job **for** **me**.
I can not quit, quit, quit!

©Ingram Publishing/SuperStock

Write About the Text

Up! Up! Up!

Pages 36-43

Eléna

I answered the question: **Why do you think the author organized the photos from day to night?**

Student Model: *Informative Text*

The author first showed things you can see in the sky during the day.
A plane is taking off.
The sun is rising.

Grammar

The words **in the sky** tell where the man is looking. It is a **prepositional phrase.**

©FogStock/Alamy

Topic
My sentences tell about what the narrator sees.

Then the author showed things in the night sky. You can see a bit of rock and gas.

I think the author wanted to show how what we see in the sky changes from day to night.

Complete Sentences
My sentence tells a complete idea.

Your Turn

COLLABORATE

Why does the narrator think that he's "in luck"? How can you tell?

Go Digital!
Write your response online.
Use your editing checklist.